Nature's Wonders

THE AMAZON RAIN FOREST

Ann Heinrichs

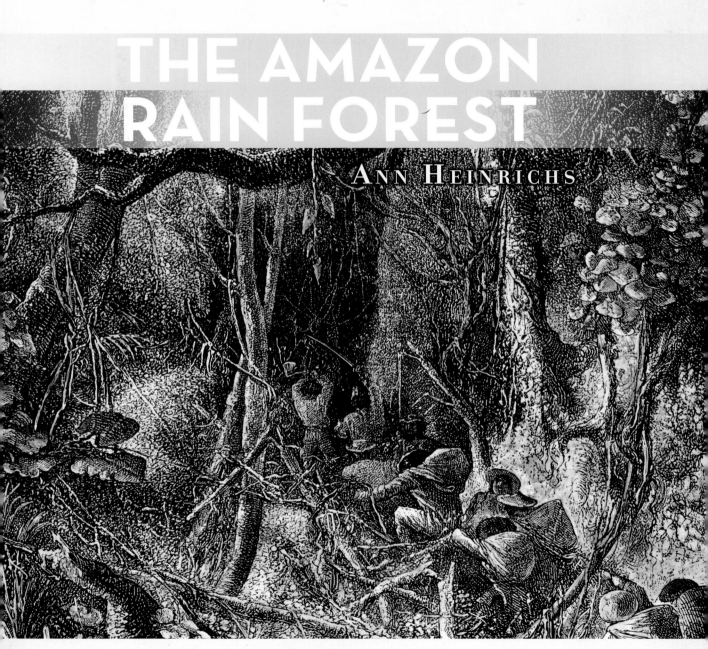

mc **Marshall Cavendish**
Benchmark
New York

Marshall Cavendish Benchmark
99 White Plains Road
Tarrytown, NY 10591
www.marshallcavendish.us

Expert Reader: Joseph A. Bishop, Ph.D., Research Associate, Department of Geography, Pennsylvania State University, State College and Chair, Science and Education Advisory Committee of the Amazon Center for Environmental Education and Research, West Chester, Pennsylvania (U.S. office)

All Internet addresses were correct and accurate at the time of printing.

Library of Congress Cataloging-in-Publication Data
Heinrichs, Ann.
The Amazon rain forest / by Ann Heinrichs.
p. cm. — (Nature's wonders)
Summary: "Provides comprehensive information on the geography, history, wildlife, peoples, and environmental issues of the Amazon Rain Forest"—Provided by publisher.
Includes bibliographical references and index.
ISBN 978-0-7614-3932-5
1. Rain forests—Amazon River Region—Juvenile literature. I. Title.
QH112.H45 2009
578.734098—dc22
2008017562

Editor: Christine Florie
Publisher: Michelle Bisson
Art Director: Anahid Hamparian
Series Designer: Kay Petronio

Photo research by Connie Gardner

Cover photo by Ricardo Siqueira/Alamy

The photographs in this book are used by permission and through the courtesy of: *Minden Pictures*: Pete Oxford, 5, 12, 29, 35, 82–83, 86; Michael and Patricia Fogden, 9, 26, 30, 39, 90(B); Claus Meyer, 15, 21, 33; Gerry Ellis, 38; Flip Nicklin, 42; Norbert Wu, 44, 90(T); Mark Moffet, 45; *Dembinsky Photo Associates*: Mark J. Thomas, 37; *Alamy*: James Brunker, 43; South American Photos, 59; Mark Downey, 65; Sue Cunningham, 76; *Corbis*: Martin Alipaz, 23; Bettmann, 56; Reuters, 63; Wolfgang Kaehler, 71; Paulo Fridman, 77; *The Image Works*: Topham, 52; *Danita Delimont*: Art Wolfe, 60; *Peter Arnold*: Jacques Jangoux, 74, 79; *Associated Press*: Alberto Cesar-Greenpeace, 11; *Digital RailRoad*: Cindy Miller Hopkins, 19; *SuperStock*: Photononstop, 18; *North Wind Picture Archive*: 46, 55; *Granger Collection*: 49; *The Image Works*: Lou Demaheis, 70.

Maps (p. 6 and p. 17) by Mapping Specialists Limited

Printed in Malaysia

1 3 5 6 4 2

CONTENTS

ONE

A Tangle of Life

Sunlight peeps through the leaves of towering trees. Brilliantly colored flowers bloom amid lush, green foliage. Howling, chirping, and buzzing sounds fill the warm, thick air. High overhead, a monkey swings on a vine as thick as your arm. Down below, a jaguar stalks its prey across the shadowy forest floor. This is the Amazon rain forest. In the words of Paul Zalis, "The Amazon is a tangle of life fighting for a piece of the sky."

The Amazon rain forest is the largest rain forest in the world. It is big enough to cover most of the continental United States. Located in northern South America, it occupies almost one-third of the South American continent. Most of the forest lies in Brazil, though it reaches into eight other countries as well.

True to its name, the Amazon rain forest is drenched by heavy rainfall. It is a tropical rain forest. That means it flourishes in Earth's tropical zone, the region closest to the equator. With intense sunlight year-round, the tropics have the world's highest temperatures. Warm, moist air in this zone rises to form rain clouds. As the air cools, it changes to rain that saturates the forest. Like all rain forests, the

The Amazon rain forest is thick with vines and lush foliage.

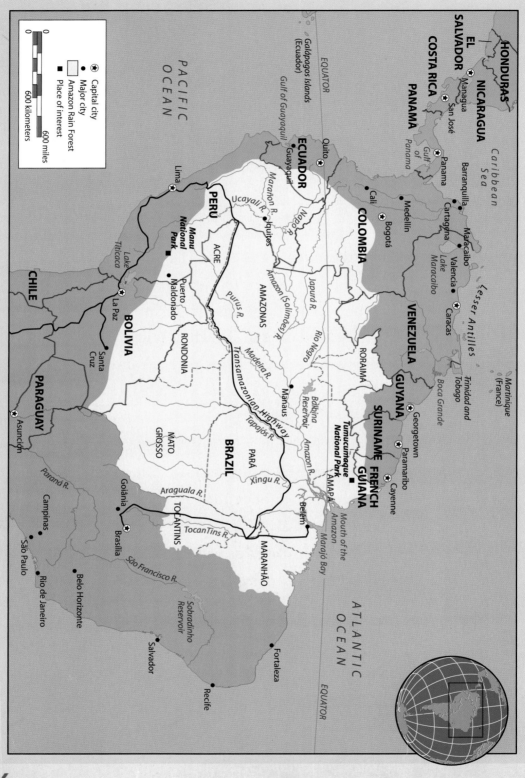

GEOPOLITICAL MAP OF THE AMAZON RAIN FOREST

Legend

- ⊛ Capital city
- • Major city
- ▢ Amazon Rain Forest
- ■ Place of interest

0 600 kilometers
0 600 miles

HONDURAS
EL SALVADOR
NICARAGUA
COSTA RICA
PANAMA
Managua
San José
Panama

Galápagos Islands (Ecuador)
Gulf of Guayaquil

PACIFIC OCEAN

EQUATOR

Caribbean Sea
Lesser Antilles
Martinique (France)

Barranquilla
Cartagena
Maracaibo
Lake Maracaibo
Valencia
Caracas
Trinidad and Tobago
Boca Grande

Quito
Guayaquil
ECUADOR
Cali
Bogotá
Medellín
COLOMBIA
VENEZUELA
GUYANA
Georgetown
SURINAME
Paramaribo
FRENCH GUIANA
Cayenne

Lima
PERU
Marañón R.
Napo R.
Ucayali R.
Iquitos
Amazon (Solimões) R.
Japurá R.
Rio Negro
AMAZONAS
RORAIMA
Tumucumaque National Park

Manu National Park
ACRE
Purus R.
Madeira R.
Manaus
Balbina Reservoir
Amazon R.
AMAPÁ
Mouth of the Amazon
Marajó Bay

La Paz
Lake Titicaca
Puerto Maldonado
RONDONIA
Transamazonian Highway
Tapajós R.
PARÁ
Belém

BOLIVIA
Santa Cruz

MATO GROSSO
BRAZIL
Xingu R.
Araguala R.
TOCANTINS
TocanTins R.
MARANHÃO

PARAGUAY
Asunción
Paraná R.

CHILE

Goiânia
Brasília
Campinas
São Paulo
Rio de Janeiro
São Francisco R.
Belo Horizonte
Sobradinho Reservoir
Salvador
Recife
Fortaleza

ATLANTIC OCEAN

EQUATOR

Amazon has a closed canopy—that is, its high treetops come together and block the sunlight.

BIODIVERSITY AND INTERDEPENDENCE

Rain forests are home to a dazzling array of animal and plant life. More than half the species on Earth thrive in these warm, moist environments. In terms of **biodiversity**, the Amazon has the richest environment of all rain forests. It contains the world's most diverse collection of animals and plants, from parrots and mahogany trees to

Tropical and Temperate Rain Forests

Tropical rain forests are rain-drenched forests near the equator. They once occupied a much larger area of the earth. Today, they are found in South and Central America, as well as central Africa, Indonesia, Malaysia, and the Philippines. More than half of all the earth's remaining rain forest is in the Amazon region.

Temperate rain forests grow in rainy areas farther from the equator. They feature cone-bearing and broadleaf evergreen trees, mosses, and ferns. Temperate rain forests can be found on the northern Pacific coast of North America, in western Chile in South America, on the east coast of Australia, and in parts of New Zealand, Japan, and Norway.

giant snakes and tiny frogs. For example, a single tree in the Amazon rain forest harbors more ant species than all of Great Britain. As many as three hundred tree species have been found on a 2.5-acre (1-hectare) plot of ground.

About 25 to 30 percent of all known plant and animal species live in the Amazon rain forest. Yet scientists have discovered only a fraction of them. Many millions of species have yet to be identified and researched. New biological studies can lead to immense benefits for humanity. Hidden within the forest is a wealth of healing substances. Many of the medicines we use today are derived from Amazon plants.

Creatures of the Amazon rain forest have adapted to their environment in unique ways. Some have webs of skin for gliding through the air, tails that

A wide variety of animal life thrives in the Amazon rain forest. One is the glasswing butterfly.

can grasp branches, or tongues that reach into a certain flower. Rain forest species depend on one another, too. For example, one type of insect may survive on just one type of leaf. Losing one key species in the food chain can be disastrous for the Amazon **ecosystem** as a whole.

EXPLOITING THE WEALTH

For thousands of years, **indigenous** people occupied the Amazon rain forest. They managed their territory wisely, taking only what they needed to survive. That fine balance began to change when Europeans first arrived in the Amazon region in the 1500s. First came the quest for gold, silver, and gemstones. In the 1800s and 1900s, merchants made fabulous fortunes from the Amazon's rubber trees. A network of roads branched out through the forest by the mid–1900s. Then outsiders reached deeper into the forest than ever before.

The Amazon's riches are still in high demand today. Miners explore for gold, oil, diamonds, and other resources. Loggers clear valuable trees, and hunters target rare animals for the illegal wildlife trade. Vast swaths of forestland are cut or burned to make way for ranches and farms.

The Amazon rain forest has undergone an alarming rate of **deforestation** over the years. With deforestation come water pollution, soil erosion, and the disappearance of species. On the human side, countless indigenous people have lost their territory, their traditional cultures, and their lives.

Deforestation is occurring at a rapid rate in the Amazon rain forest. Here, acres of rain forest have been cleared to make way for soybean fields.

Today, people around the world are trying to save the rain forest. Scientists and environmental groups are carrying out countless projects in the Amazon region. Working with government agencies, they hope to halt the damage, to help the forest recover, and to keep it alive for generations to come.

TWO

A River Runs through It

The Amazon rain forest stretches across northern South America. The equator cuts through its northern edge. This lush, tropical forest reaches into nine of South America's twelve countries. Most of the forest—about 60 percent—lies in Brazil. Large tracts of forest also flourish in Venezuela, Colombia, Peru, Ecuador, and Bolivia. The forest spreads into Guyana, Suriname, and French Guiana, too.

Millions of years ago, a great freshwater sea covered what is now the Amazon rain forest. Today, the forest still occupies a vast lowland. The high Andes Mountains mark the forest's western boundary. This mountain range runs down South America's western edge. On the east, the forest reaches as far as Brazil's Atlantic coast. The Guiana Highlands border the forest in the north. This mountainous region runs from southeastern Venezuela across Guyana, Suriname, French Guiana, and northern Brazil. To the south are the hilly Brazilian Highlands.

◄ *A dugout canoe navigates through one of many waterways in the Amazon rain forest.*

THE AMAZON RIVER

Coursing through the rain forest is the mighty Amazon River. Its waters rise high in the Andes Mountains of Peru. Here, the Marañón and Ucayali rivers gather water from the icy slopes. They rush through gorges, plunge over waterfalls, and descend through the foothills of the Andes into the lowlands of the Amazon rain forest. At last the two rivers join to form the Amazon River near Nauta, Peru. From there the Amazon winds its way eastward across Brazil. After a journey of about 4,000 miles (6,440 kilometers), the great river empties at last into the Atlantic Ocean near Belém, Brazil. Brazilians call the river the Solimões before it reaches the city of Manaus. From Manaus to the ocean, they call it the Amazon.

There are more than one thousand rivers in the Amazon rain forest. Here, one of ▶▶ them snakes through dense vegetation.

Traditionally, the Amazon River has been called the second-longest river in the world, after Africa's Nile River. Measurements taken in 2007 indicate that the Amazon may be longer than the Nile. These findings are not yet widely accepted by geographers, however. In terms of water volume, the Amazon is the world's largest river. At its widest point, the Amazon is 7 miles (11 km) wide during the dry season and 28 miles (45 km) wide during the rainy season. It carries about one-fifth of all the water that flows into the earth's oceans. More than 50 million gallons (189 million liters) of water gush from its mouth every second! This immense volume of water runs off millions of acres of land.

More than a thousand rivers run through the Amazon rain forest. Most are **tributaries** of the Amazon River and join it along its course. Together, these rivers gather waters from about 2.7 million square miles (7 million sq km) of land. This area is called the Amazon River Basin, or Amazonia. It is the largest river basin in the world. The Amazon rain forest occupies most of that basin.

BLACKWATER, WHITEWATER, AND CLEARWATER

Twelve of the Amazon's tributaries are more than 1,000 miles (1,600 km) long. The longest is the Madeira River, whose waters rise in the Bolivian Andes. Then the Madeira snakes its way through central Brazil before joining the Amazon east of Manaus. Other long tributaries include the Purus, which rises in Peru, and the Japurá,

PHYSICAL MAP OF THE AMAZON RAIN FOREST

Elevation

Feet	Meters
Over 10,000	Over 3,048
5,000–10,000	1,524–3,048
2,000–5,000	610–1,524
1,000–2,000	305–610
500–1,000	152–305
0–500	0–152
Below Sea Level	Below Sea Level

⊛ Capital city

600 miles
600 kilometers

ATLANTIC OCEAN

Cape Branco

Sobradinho Reservoir

São Francisco R.

BRAZILIAN HIGHLANDS

Brasília ⊛

Tocantins R.

Araguaia R.

Paraná R.

BRAZIL

Xingu R.

Mouths of the Amazon

Marajó Bay

Amazon R.

MATO GROSSO PLATEAU

Tapajós R.

Asunción ⊛

PARAGUAY

Madeira R.

Balbina Reservoir

Black R. (Rio Negro)

Pico da Neblina 9,888 ft (3,014 m)

Japurá R.

AMAZON RIVER

BASIN

Purus R.

Juruá R.

Sucre ⊛

BOLIVIA

La Paz ⊛

Lake Titicaca

ANDES MOUNTAINS

CHILE

Amazon (Solimões) R.

Cayenne ⊛

Paramaribo ⊛

FRENCH GUIANA

SURINAME

Georgetown ⊛

GUYANA

Boca Grande

Martinique (France)

Lesser Antilles

Caracas ⊛

VENEZUELA

GUIANA HIGHLANDS

LLANOS

Lake Maracaibo

Bogotá ⊛

COLOMBIA

Caribbean Sea

Panama ⊛

Gulf of Panama

PANAMA

San José ⊛

COSTA RICA

Managua ⊛

NICARAGUA

HONDURAS

EL SALVADOR

Quito ⊛

ECUADOR

Galápagos Islands (Ecuador)

Gulf of Guayaquil

Aguja Point

Marañón R.

Ucayali R.

Lima ⊛

PERU

PACIFIC OCEAN

A River Runs through It **17**

which begins in Colombia. The Rio Negro is considered the Amazon's largest tributary. Although it is not as long as some other tributaries, it carries the largest volume of water. The Rio Negro is about 5 miles (8 km) wide when it joins the Amazon near Manaus.

The Rio Negro is known as a blackwater river. It gets its tea-colored hue from decaying plant material that it picks up along its course. Many whitewater rivers feed into the Amazon, too. They get their creamy-brown shade from light-colored clay that they absorb in the Andes Mountains. The Amazon River itself is a whitewater river, and the Madeira and Purus rivers are two of its whitewater tributaries.

The Amazon River's largest tributary is the dark-watered Rio Negro.

Finally, there are clearwater rivers, with crystal-clear, blue-green waters. They originate in the Guiana Highlands in the north and the Brazilian Highlands in the south. The Xingu and Tapajós are two of the Amazon Basin's clearwater rivers.

The Wedding of the Waters

The contrast between the Amazon region's blackwater and whitewater rivers is most astonishing at Manaus. Here, the dark waters of the Rio Negro meet the light waters of the Amazon River. This spot is sometimes called the Wedding of the Waters. The two colors are strikingly visible for miles until they eventually blend together.

HUMIDITY, RAINFALL, AND FLOODS

Walk through the rain forest, and the air feels heavy, thick, and wet. That is due to the high level of humidity, or moisture in the air. This airborne moisture has two main sources—**evaporation** and **transpiration**.

Heavy rainfall drenches the forest and, due to the high temperature, much of the water evaporates into the air. As a whole, the Amazon rain forest receives an average of about 90 inches (230 centimeters) of rainfall a year. Rainfall varies by region, though, with various areas averaging from 60 to 120 inches (150 to 300 cm) of rainfall every year. In contrast, the U.S. state of Iowa averages about 34 inches (86 cm) of precipitation a year.

The rain forest itself generates about half of its own rainfall. Through a process called transpiration, plant leaves release

◀ *Vapor rises over the Amazon rain forest as dawn approaches.*

water **vapor** into the atmosphere. This moisture returns as rainfall. It is estimated that trees release 200 gallons (760 liters) of water into the air every year through transpiration. That water, in the form of vapor, rises to create rain clouds that drench the forest again.

Although the Amazon rain forest receives rain year-round, it has a rainy season and a dry, or less-rainy, season. The rainy season, called summer, lasts from roughly November through May. This season does not begin at the same time throughout the region. Heavy rains begin in mid-October in the western Amazon and gradually move eastward. In the far-eastern Amazon, the rains begin in December.

During the rainy season, the rivers flood. Animals leave for higher ground, and fish swim into the flooded river valleys to eat fruits and seeds from the underwater trees. In June, the waters begin to recede and the dry season, called winter, begins. Surprisingly, the forest is actually greener during the dry season. This is because the days are sunnier and, after the rains, the trees' longer roots find moisture deep in the ground.

TEMPERATURE

The Amazon rain forest is warm year-round, but it is not terribly hot. The high humidity makes it seem warmer than it is. Temperatures in the forest average about 79 degrees Fahrenheit (26 °Celsius). The rainy season is cooler than the dry season, and nights are cooler than days. However, the difference between nighttime and daytime temperatures is greater than any seasonal differences.

Cattle gather on a strip of dry Amazon lowland after heavy rains flood the region.

FLOODPLAINS AND SOILS

Broad lowlands lie alongside the Amazon River and its tributaries. These lowlands are flooded during the rainy season. This creates a **floodplain** as wide as 30 miles (48 km). The rivers may rise as high as 50 feet (15 meters), leaving only the treetops above the waterline. When the waters recede, they leave behind **silt**, which enriches the soil with valuable nutrients. Floodplains along blackwater and clear-water rivers are typically called *igapó*, while whitewater floodplains are called *várzea*.

These fertile floodplains, or flooded forests, make up only a small portion of the Amazon rain forest. Most of the forest occupies higher ground called *terra firme*, Portuguese for "solid land." High bluffs rise from the floodplain up to the terra firme. In some places, the annual floodwaters gouge out the sides of the bluffs. This creates *terra caída*, or "fallen land," where a chunk of the forest above has fallen into the river below.

Looking at the lush plant life in the rain forest, it might seem that all its soils are rich and fertile. However, most of the forest's soil is thin and low in nutrients. This is because the annual floods do not reach the higher ground to deposit minerals there. Most of the soil in the rain forest gets its nutrients from plants decaying on the forest floor.

OXYGEN, CARBON DIOXIDE, AND CLIMATE CHANGE

The Amazon rain forest has been called the lungs of the earth. It actually helps the planet to breathe. When people and animals breathe, they inhale oxygen and exhale carbon dioxide. Trees and other plants work the opposite way. They take in carbon dioxide and give off oxygen. Together, these two processes make up what is called the biological carbon cycle.

By taking in carbon dioxide, the rain forest helps recycle the air and keep it clean. With its billions of trees, the forest releases a tremendous amount of oxygen into the atmosphere. It is estimated that the Amazon rain forest produces more than 20 percent of the world's oxygen. This is vital in keeping the earth's life forms in balance.

Modern civilization challenges that balance, though. Exhausts from vehicles and industrial plants pour tons of carbon dioxide and other chemicals into the air. The forest cannot process this overload of gases. The excess carbon dioxide remains in the atmosphere, encircling the globe and causing temperatures to rise worldwide.

Deforestation upsets the balance, too. Loggers cut down many acres of rain forest trees every day. Native populations clear more trees for farming, usually by burning vast areas of forestland. These activities do more than remove trees from the recycling process. Decaying trees and smoke from the fires release even more carbon dioxide into the atmosphere. In time, the Amazon rain forest could give out more carbon dioxide than it absorbs. This would have a serious impact on climate conditions in the rain forest, in surrounding areas, and around the planet. Scientists are monitoring this situation by keeping a close eye on the forest's carbon dioxide levels, temperature, and rainfall.

THREE

Into the Wild

Monkeys howl and scream from the treetops. Birds screech among the branches, and frogs chirp in the shade of a fragrant flower. Snakes dangle like vines from a tree limb, and insects scurry along the forest floor. The Amazon rain forest is a world of its own, with unmistakable sights, sounds, and smells. It's alive, noisy, and always in motion.

Many separate ecosystems exist within the Amazon rain forest. Each ecosystem is a dynamic community of plants and animals. They work together as a unit, interacting with one another and depending on one another for survival. Each plant and animal in the ecosystem plays a role in the others' survival, and this keeps the whole ecosystem in balance.

THE FOREST LAYERS

One way to study the Amazon's ecosystems is to look at the forest's layers. Scientists divide the Amazon rain forest into four layers.

◀ *A tiger-striped leaf frog clings to a heliconia plant in the Amazon rain forest.*

From top to bottom, they are the overstory, the canopy, the under-story, and the forest floor. (Some scientists describe five layers. They divide the understory into a tree layer and a shrub layer.) Each layer has its own community of plants and animals. In fact, some creatures spend their entire lives in just one layer of the forest.

THE OVERSTORY

The forest's tallest trees form the overstory, also called the emer-gent layer. Scattered here and there, these massive trees emerge as high as 100 feet (30 m) above the rest of the forest. Reaching toward the sunlight, they have been able to pierce through the thick canopy below. Some of them grow taller than 200 feet (60 m). At this level, the climate is much different than in the forest below, with drier air and strong winds. Many trees in the overstory have buttress roots, or prop roots. These open-air root systems spread out at the base of the tree. They keep high winds from blowing the trees down. One of the tallest overstory trees is the kapok, or silk-cotton, tree. Its seeds are attached to fluffy fibers that people use to stuff pillows. These windblown fibers carry the seeds for miles.

Birds of prey build their nests in the overstory. From on high, they can spot animals in the canopy and swoop down to snatch them. The harpy eagle is an enormous predator. It grows as long as 3 feet (1 m), with a 6-foot (2-m) wingspan. It targets large animals such as monkeys, sloths, kinkajous, and parrots. Bats, butterflies, and some monkeys inhabit the overstory, too.

A harpy eagle perches on the branch of a kapok tree in the Amazon's overstory.

THE CANOPY

The dense canopy forms a kind of ceiling or roof for the forest. Canopy trees rise about 100 to 130 feet (30 to 40 m) above the forest floor. The trees grow closely together, and their leafy tree-tops block out almost all the sunlight from the forest below. About 90 percent of the rain forest's animals live in the canopy, including millions of insect species. Many animals never leave the canopy. Leaping or gliding from branch to branch, they can travel for miles across the high foliage without ever touching the ground.

Canopy trees include Brazil nut, fig, rubber, mahogany, and hundreds of species of palm trees. As with trees in the overstory, mahogany trees

have large buttress roots to keep them stable. Birds, bats, monkeys, and dozens of other animals feed on fruits, nuts, and seeds in the canopy. These animals help grow new trees by depositing the seeds in their droppings far away.

Trees in the canopy are bristling with epiphytes. Sometimes called air plants, epiphytes anchor themselves to tree trunks and branches. They take no nutrients from the trees. Instead, they live on air, rain, and decaying plant matter. Orchids and bromeliads, such as pineapples, are common epiphytes in the Amazon.

Lianas are long, woody vines that wind their way through the canopy. Monkeys swing on lianas as they move through the treetops. Lianas are rooted in the forest floor. They

◀◀ *Red and green macaws hang from a liana in the canopy of the Amazon.*

gradually make their way up the tree trunks into the upper branches. Then they spread from one tree to another, providing a bridge for animals and insects. Epiphytes and lianas can weigh a tree down and even cause it to fall over.

A Walk through the Canopy

Few people ever get a glimpse of life in the canopy. But visitors can explore the canopy world at Inkaterra Reserva Amazónica (Inkaterra Ecological Reserve) in Puerto Maldonado, Peru. Visitors climb up to the Canopy Walkway, a 1,135-foot (346-m) network of walkways and hanging bridges, 100 feet (30 m) above the forest floor. The walkways, treetop platforms, and observation towers provide a rare view of the canopy **habitat**, where most of the rain forest species live.

The Understory and the Forest Floor

The understory is sometimes called the lower canopy. It consists of shorter tree species and young trees that have not yet grown up to the canopy level. Cecropia trees, with their umbrella-shaped leaf pattern, are common trees in the understory. Called ant plants, they harbor colonies of ants that protect the tree by attacking insects, animals, and vines that approach it. Fast-growing cecropias are the first species to move into a forest area that has been cut. Cocoa trees are common understory trees, too. Their seeds are made into cocoa and chocolate. Beneath the trees are bushy plants that grow as high as 5 to 20 feet (1.5 to 6 m) above the ground.

Many plants in the understory have large leaves that capture as much sunlight as possible. Many also have bright flowers that attract bees, butterflies, hummingbirds, and wasps. The insects carry pollen from one flower to another, thus enabling the plants to reproduce. Snakes, lizards, and frogs creep along the branches and leaves. Many birds build their nests in the understory, and some monkeys hunt for food there, too. Jaguars often climb into the understory to get a good view of prey below.

The floor of the Amazon rain forest is a shadowy world. Since so little light reaches the ground, few plants grow there. However, the ground is rich in nutrients from rotting plants, decaying animals, and animal waste. Many kinds of fungi live on the forest floor, as well as worms and other insects. They help the decaying process by decomposing the material.

A jaguar waits in the understory for its next meal.

When a tree falls, sunlight suddenly streams in on a patch of the forest floor. This is called a light gap. Competing for sunlight, many plants move in to fill the gap. First come shrubs, vines, and fast-growing understory trees such as cecropia, balsa, and bamboo. They are soon overtaken by the hardy seedlings of canopy trees, whose growth is stimulated by the sunlight.

Medicinal Plants: Finding the Cures

Indigenous people have used plants to treat medical problems for thousands of years. People outside the Amazon are beginning to discover these healing substances, too. One-fourth of all the medicines people use today contain ingredients derived from rain forest plants.

One medicinal plant is the cinchona tree. Its bark produces quinine, a chemical used to treat malaria. Another healing substance is curare, which comes from a woody vine. Some indigenous people use curare to poison arrows and darts. Surgeons once used it as a muscle relaxant during surgery. Now they use a synthetic form of curare.

The National Cancer Institute regularly tests rain forest species. It has identified more than two thousand rain forest plants that have cancer-fighting properties. Many drug companies are also researching rain forest plants. Given time—and the survival of the forest—researchers may find cures for the world's most deadly diseases.

MONKEYS

Howler monkeys are the loudest creatures in the canopy. Early explorers were terrified when they first heard howler monkeys. They were afraid some terrible monster was about to attack. True to their name, howler monkeys have a blood-curdling howl that can be heard up to 3 miles (5 km) away. Howler monkeys' tails are prehensile—that is, they can curl around and grasp objects such as branches. Traveling in troops of up to thirty, they feed together within a certain territory.

Capuchin monkeys travel through the canopy in noisy troops. They eat not only fruits, seeds, and flower nectar, but also caterpillars, frogs, lizards, and even baby birds.

Spider monkeys are agile little monkeys that swing around the treetops using their long limbs and tail and leap

Howler monkeys, with their distinct howl, are common throughout the canopy.

from tree to tree. They live in the canopy and drink the water that collects in bromeliads. The saki is sometimes called the flying monkey. It can leap more than 30 feet (10 m) between trees.

Tamarins and marmosets are some of the smallest monkeys.

Their long, bushy tails do not curl or grasp. They eat fruits, berries, insects, and bird eggs. The endangered golden lion tamarin is known for its long, golden fur. Pygmy marmosets are the world's smallest monkeys. An adult's body, not counting the tail, is about 6 inches (15 cm) long.

BIRDS

More than 1,300 bird species live in the Amazon rain forest. Many rain forest birds are brilliantly colored and have loud calls. Parrots are a perfect example. Various species have bright red, yellow, blue, or green feathers. Most species travel in flocks and fill the treetops with noisy screeches. Parrots have strong beaks that can crack seeds and nuts. They also use their beaks as a kind of third foot to help them climb around the trees.

Macaws are a type of parrot. The scarlet macaw, with its brilliant red plumage, inhabits both the overstory and the canopy. Some macaws are picky eaters. They travel hundreds of miles to find the food they want. Macaws and other parrots are popular as pets, and they sell for high prices. As a result, their populations have been reduced drastically.

The keel-billed toucan's enormous beak can measure up to one-third of the bird's total length. Toucans do not often fly. Instead, they hop from branch to branch. They eat fruit, insects, and small animals such as tree frogs. Yellow-rumped caciques build nests in colonies of as many as one hundred nests. The females do the building before they mate. Antbirds exhibit a very specialized behavior. They follow trails of army ants along the ground. Instead of eating the ants, they eat the insects that scurry to escape the ants.

OTHER TREE DWELLERS

Three-toed sloths live in both the understory and the canopy. They spend almost 80 percent of their time napping. To sleep, sloths often hang upside down from a tree branch with all four legs, gripping it with their long, curved claws. About once or twice a week, they climb down to the base of the tree to urinate and defecate.

Coatis—also called coatimundis—live in the canopy but also spend some time on the forest floor. They

The toucan is a bird that rarely flies. It hops from branch to branch as it looks for food.

eat worms, lizards, fruits, and nuts. With their double-jointed ankles, they can climb down trees headfirst.

The tamandua is an anteater that spends most of its time in the trees. It grips branches with its prehensile tail and claws its way into ant or termite nests. The tree-dwelling porcupine also has a prehensile tail. So does the kinkajou, a raccoon relative that comes out to eat at night.

More than one thousand frog species live in the Amazon rain forest. They spend most of their time in the canopy or the understory. Most of them are bright and shiny. The poison-dart, or poison-arrow, frog can be green, yellow, red, orange, or brilliant blue. Indigenous people use the **toxic** substance in the frog's skin to poison the tips of their darts and arrows. The emerald tree boa lives in the trees, too. This snake's color protects it from predators and hides it from potential prey. Even humans often pass by without noticing it.

The emerald tree boa blends in with its natural surroundings.

The Amazon region is home to more than nine hundred species of bats. One is the vampire bat. With its sharp teeth, it tears a hole in an animal's skin. Then it licks the blood that oozes out. Fruit bats feed on fruits and nectar in the canopy, the overstory, and the understory.

ROAMING THE FOREST FLOOR

Jaguars are stealthy hunters. They often hunt by night, lying in wait near riverbanks and pouncing on large animals that come to drink. These good swimmers will dive into the water after prey. Tough skins or turtle shells are no obstacles for the jaguar. Its powerful jaws can crunch through them easily.

Tapirs are the largest mammals in the Amazon rain forest. They look like huge, brown pigs and have a large proboscis—something like an elephant's trunk, only shorter. The proboscis helps the tapir push plants into its mouth. A similar animal, the peccary, is a wild, hairy pig with tusks.

Capybaras are the world's largest rodents. They look somewhat like guinea pigs, but they weigh up to 150 pounds (70 kilograms). The agouti is a smaller rodent about the size of a rabbit. It eats many

The largest mammal in the Amazon rain forest is the tapir.

of the fruits and nuts that fall down from the canopy. Agoutis can cut Brazil nuts open with their sharp teeth.

Many small deer species graze on the forest floor. They are a favorite prey for jaguars. Bush dogs are ferocious little predators that are also good swimmers. They hunt rodents and other small animals.

An Insect's World

Visitors to the Amazon rain forest often see a string of upright leaves that seem to be marching across the forest floor. This is really a column of leaf-cutter ants. Some leaf-cutter ants climb high into the canopy and cut off leaf fragments. Down below, other ants march single-file as they carry the leaves back to their underground nest. In the nest, they chew the leaves and use them to fertilize gardens of fungus, the ants' primary food.

Army ants are aggressive. They attack and eat insects, lizards, frogs, baby birds, and other small animals. Azteca ants live only on cecropia trees. They attack other insects on the tree and eat vines and epiphytes that begin to grow there. As a result, the trees have nothing preventing them from growing to their full potential.

These are just a few of the Amazon's hundreds of ant species. No one knows how many species live there. New species are being discovered all the time. One scientist in Peru's Reserva Amazónica counted 362 species in that one area alone.

The forest floor is also home to many arachnids, members of the spider family. One amazing species is the goliath bird eater. This giant tarantula is the biggest spider in the world. With their legs extended, bird eaters measure up to 12 inches (30 cm). They pounce on their prey and bite it with their large fangs. Despite their name, they mostly eat insects, lizards, frogs, and mice rather than birds.

Other insects spend their time in the canopy. The brilliant blue morpho butterfly feeds on fruit and nectar. The fig wasp lays its eggs inside a fig so its young will have food to eat. Male orchid bees enter a certain kind of orchid to pick up its perfume, which attracts female orchid bees for mating.

WATER CREATURES

More than three thousand fish species live in the Amazon's waters. During flood season, many of them feed on the fruits and seeds of flooded trees. Thus, they act as seed dispersers, helping to spread tree species far across the forest.

The red-bellied piranha, with its razor-sharp teeth, can easily chomp through large animal bones. Most of the Amazon's twenty piranha species are vegetarians, though. One of the Amazon's strangest fish is a giant, air-breathing fish called the pirarucu. It begins life with gills, which fish use to breathe. Then it gradually develops a lunglike organ for breathing air. About once every ten minutes, it comes up out of the water to breathe.

Anacondas inhabit the Amazon's rivers and swamps. These gigantic snakes grow up to 30 feet (9 m) long. However, there have been unconfirmed reports of 60-foot (18-m) anacondas. They are in close competition with pythons for the title of largest snake species in the world. The anaconda does not bite its prey. Instead, it coils itself around an animal and crushes it. Then it swallows the animal whole, which can take many hours for larger animals.

Manatees are the Amazon's largest aquatic mammal, growing up to 9 feet (3 m) long. Another water mammal is the Amazon river dolphin, also known as the pink dolphin or *boto.* It is the world's largest freshwater dolphin. Caimans, small relatives of the alligator, glide through the water searching for food. Electric eels, turtles, and giant river otters make their homes in the waterways, too.

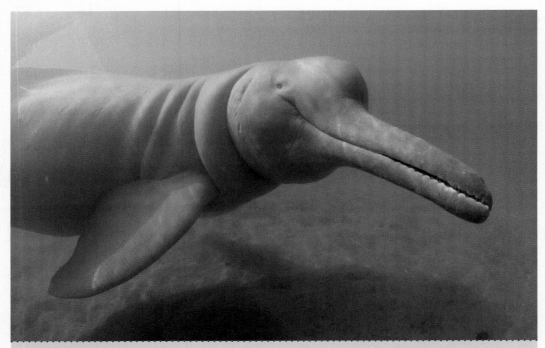

Most dolphins live in salt water. However, the Amazon river dolphin makes its home in the fresh waters of the Amazon.

The Giant River Otter

Giant river otters are enormous members of the weasel family. They can grow up to 7 feet (2 m) long and weigh up to 70 pounds (32 kg). Their Spanish nickname is *lobos de río*, or river wolves, because of their wolflike teeth. With whiskers that sense water currents and front feet with webbed membranes, giant otters are powerful swimmers and hunters. They hunt alone or in packs of four to ten adults, mostly preying on fish. However, they have been known to devour anacondas and caimans, too. Giant river otters were hunted for their skins until only a few thousand remained in the wild. They are now one of the Amazon's most endangered species.

In a symbiotic relationship, algae grows on the coat of this tree sloth, giving it a greenish tint.

INTERDEPENDENCE IN SMALL PLACES

Just one small area of the rain forest can provide a habitat for hundreds of species. Some bromeliads, called tank bromeliads, are a good example. Their stiff, curved leaves form cups in which pools of rainwater gather. Some species can hold more than 12 gallons (45 liters) of water! These pools are entire ecosystems. Algae and bacteria grow in the water, and insects feed on them. Frogs eat the insects, and snakes, birds, and larger frogs eat the smaller frogs.

Certain frogs, called bromeliad frogs, deposit their eggs or tadpoles in the pool. An example is the poison-dart frog, which lays its eggs among moist leaves on the forest floor. When the eggs hatch into tadpoles, the adult carries the tadpoles on its back up the tree, a few at a time. It climbs up to a bromeliad, deposits the tadpoles in the pool, and then climbs back down to get more tadpoles.

Sloths provide another small-scale ecosystem, as they live in a **symbiotic** relationship with several species. Blue-green algae grow in their fur, giving the sloths a blotchy, greenish look. This color-ation protects the sloth by blending in with its surroundings. Moths,

This poison-dart frog has deposited its tadpole into a pool of water that has collected in a bromeliad.

beetles, mites, and many other insects live in sloths' fur, too. One sloth may be home to a thousand beetles!

In another type of symbiosis, some rain forest species cannot survive without others. For example, the female orchid bee is the only insect that can pollinate Brazil nut trees. It has a tongue long enough to reach into the tree's coiled flower, where it picks up pollen. Brazil nut trees grown outside the forest do not reproduce well. These are just a few examples of the complex interrelationships within the Amazon rain forest.

FOUR

From Exploration to Exploitation

Spanish and Portuguese explorers were the first Europeans to explore the Amazon rain forest. They arrived in the 1500s. At that time, European powers were competing for a foothold in the Americas. Explorers such as Christopher Columbus had sailed west from Europe, hoping to reach Asian lands they called the Indies. In the Indies there were spices and other exotic trade goods that fetched high prices in European markets. Instead, the explorers reached the Americas, where they called the native people Indians. This New World, they imagined, held riches of its own. Legends told of golden cities and other fabulous treasures to be discovered.

The Spanish and Portuguese began to collide in South America. So, through the 1494 Treaty of Tordesillas, South America was divided up. The Portuguese could explore and colonize the eastern part of the continent. This eventually covered today's Brazil, including most of the Amazon rain forest. Spain got western South America, including Peru, Colombia, Ecuador, Venezuela, and Bolivia. Thus,

◀ *The first European explorers of the Amazon rain forest arrived during the 1500s.*

Brazil became a Portuguese-speaking country, while the rest of the continent spoke Spanish.

Explorers' first forays into the Amazon rain forest were expeditions on the Amazon River. In 1500 Spaniard Vicente Yáñez Pinzón became the first European to sail into the river. This waterway was the first "highway" into the forest. As they sailed down the river, explorers encountered the dense forest, its wildlife, and the people who made their homes there.

THE SEARCH FOR GOLD AND CINNAMON

Legends of El Dorado stirred the imaginations of explorers. Indians had told them of this wondrous land, where the chief was covered in gold dust. He washed it off in a lake, into which his subjects also cast golden objects. Just as intriguing was the tale of La Canela, the Land of Cinnamon. According to the Indians, vast groves of cinnamon trees lay somewhere east of the Andes Mountains. Cinnamon, an exotic spice of the Indies, had made fortunes for many a trader.

Greedy and ruthless, Spaniard Gonzalo Pizarro was determined to find these lands. His half brother, Francisco Pizarro, had conquered the Inca Empire of Peru in the 1530s. Now Pizarro wanted an empire of his own. In 1541 he became the Spanish governor of Quito, today's capital of Ecuador. At once he set out to explore the fabled lands. He forced four thousand Indians into service as porters.

Pizarro's second in command was Francisco de Orellana. Following the Napo River, a tributary of the Amazon, the two became separated. Pizarro grew impatient and returned to Quito, while Orellana continued on.

We learned what happened to Orellana from the writings of Gaspar de Carvajal, a Spanish priest who joined the expedition. The travelers ran out of supplies and were forced to eat "leather, belts, and soles of shoes cooked with certain herbs." Most of the Indians died of hunger and poor treatment. As his party floated down the river, Orellana engaged in several battles with Indians, who fought with clubs and bows and arrows.

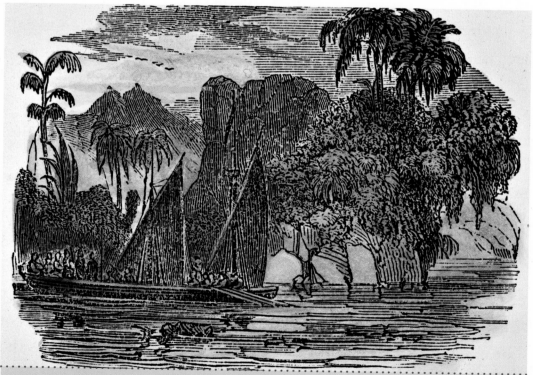

Francisco de Orellana and his crew sail down the Amazon River in search of the riches claimed to be in the region.

The grass-skirted warriors in one village, Orellana said, were women. He called them Amazons, after the female warriors of ancient Greek legends. Orellana's Amazons may simply have been long-haired men. In any case, it was Orellana who gave the name to the river and the entire forested region. When Orellana reached the mouth of the river in 1542, he became the first European to travel the length of the Amazon River.

Soon other countries began sending expeditions into the Amazon. By the 1600s the Dutch had built forts on the river. In 1620 English captain Roger North led a group of English and Irish explorers up the Amazon. They planned to establish a tobacco plantation and to collect spices and rare woods. One of North's men, Irishman Bernard O'Brien, established his own settlement. All these settlers recruited thousands of Indians to work their land and to guard their forts.

In time, the Portuguese felt they had to establish their claim on the Amazon. In 1639 Portuguese adventurer Pedro Teixeira traveled upriver from Belém to Quito. He battled all foreigners along the way. He was the first European to travel the entire Amazon upstream, from east to west.

On the way back, Teixeira brought a priest named Cristóbal de Acuña. His journal is the first published description of the Amazon. Acuña described the region as a paradise. He wrote that "the river is full of fish, the forests of game, the air of birds, the trees are covered with fruit, the plains with corn, the earth is rich in mines, and the natives have such skill and ability."

Men of Science

Explorers and fortune seekers were not the only people interested in the Amazon region. Scientists wanted to study the forest's rich animal and plant life. In 1735 the French Academy of Sciences sent Charles-Marie de La Condamine to South America to take geographical measurements at the equator. He ended up spending nine years in the Amazon region.

La Condamine drew remarkably accurate maps. He also reported on amazing plants and animals, as well as Indian culture. One plant substance he studied was curare, a poison the Indians used on their arrow tips. Another was latex, the milky sap of the rubber tree, which he took back to Europe. He also took cinchona plants, with their valuable quinine.

Baron Alexander von Humboldt has been called "the last great universal man." A wealthy German nobleman, Humboldt was also a natural scientist, a geographer, and a tireless explorer. He measured and collected everything. In 1799 he set out for South America with French botanist Aimé Bonpland. During their five-year expedition, they collected 60,000 plant specimens, as well as rocks, animal skins, and Indian artifacts from the Amazon Basin. Humboldt published a thirty-volume report on his studies.

Many more scientists explored the mysteries of the Amazon rain forest. One was Charles Darwin. As a young scientist exploring the forest in 1832, he took long walks to collect specimens. He sent

Alexander von Humboldt and Aimé Bonpland spent five years in the Amazon exploring its wonders.

loads of bird, mammal, fish, insect, and plant specimens back to England to study when he returned. Darwin was amazed to see how plants and animals adapted to their environment and formed new species in the process. These studies led to his theory of evolution.

Henry Walter Bates and Alfred Russel Wallace were British scientists who specialized in insects. They took off for the Amazon in 1848. Wallace stayed for four years, but Bates spent eleven years there, as he cataloged more than 14,000 species. Focusing on butterflies, he discovered a type of imitation that was named after him—Batesian mimicry. It involves a harmless species of butterfly developing the colors and markings of a bad-tasting or poisonous butterfly. This helps keep the harmless butterfly safe from predators.

THE RUBBER BOOM

In the 1880s people began to exploit the Amazon rain forest's rubber trees. Indians had been extracting latex from the trees for centuries. Once rubber became desirable in European markets, businessmen looked to the Amazon as a rich source of rubber, which they called black gold. Wealthy merchants called rubber barons began massive rubber operations, using Indians as slave laborers. Manaus became the capital of the rubber region. Belém, near the mouth of the Amazon River, and Iquitos, in Peru, prospered, too. These cities had electricity, running water, and sewers long before the rest of the region did.

Massive wealth poured into Manaus, where many of the rubber barons lived. They built luxurious homes and magnificent public

Native Indians in the Amazon tapped rubber trees for merchants who became wealthy from the rubber trade.

buildings such as the Teatro Amazonas. This ornate opera house was built in grand European style, with crystal chandeliers from France and marble from Italy. Manaus was a center for the diamond industry, too, as diamonds could be extracted from the forest. During this time, nearly 40 percent of Brazil's exports came from the Amazon region.

The rubber boom died down by about 1912. Back in the 1870s, English explorer Henry Wickham had smuggled 70,000 rubber tree seeds out of the Amazon, and the British had planted them in their colony in Malaysia. The Malaysian plantations became so efficient that the Amazon rubber market collapsed. It had a brief revival during World War II (1939–1945) but declined to a small industry again.

NATION BUILDING AND DEFORESTATION

Brazil became an independent republic in 1889. As part of its nation-building plan, the new republic marched ahead to develop and modernize its economy. Cândido Rondon, a military engineer, was assigned to put up telegraph lines in the Amazon region. In the process, he cleared roads, explored new territory, discovered unknown rivers, and made contact with many Indian peoples. Brazil's Rondônia state, most of which is in the Amazon rain forest, was named after him.

In 1964 the Brazilian military took control of the government. Then the push for modernization went into high gear. Thousands of

Explorer and Humanitarian

Cândido Mariano da Silva Rondon (1865–1958) was Brazil's greatest native explorer. As an army engineer, he spent years setting up telegraph lines through unexplored regions of Brazil's interior. In 1914 he and former U.S. president Theodore Roosevelt took a scientific expedition together. They explored a river that Rondon had discovered earlier—the River of Doubt, which was renamed Río Roosevelt.

Rondon's mother had been a Bororo Indian, and he treated Indians with courtesy and care. He was horrified by the inhumane treatment they received at the hands of white people. In 1910 he helped establish Brazil's Indian Protection Service (SPI) and became its first director. He worked to protect the Indians' territory and culture and to help them economically. In 1952 Rondon established Xingu National Park, Brazil's first Indian reservation. Admired as both an explorer and a humanitarian, Rondon became a national hero.

The Trans-Amazon Highway was built in the hopes of creating an economically active region in the Amazon.

square miles of forest were cleared to build roads across the Amazon Basin. Dams for hydroelectric power were built across rivers, and massive areas of the forest were flooded. The government gave financial benefits to people who settled in the Amazon wilderness. Farmers, cattle ranchers, and loggers poured in. They felled trees and burned forestland.

In the late 1970s, large gold deposits were discovered on the Yanomami people's land near the Brazil–Venezuela border. This sparked a gold rush that is still going on today. Thousands of *garimpeiros*, or gold prospectors, swarmed over the territory, and they killed anyone who got in their way. The search for mahogany trees, diamonds, oil, and other valuable resources brought more violence and destruction to the region.

A New Breed of Explorers

The devastation of the Amazon rain forest and its people came to worldwide attention in the 1980s. Human-rights groups, university researchers, and international organizations such as the World Wildlife Fund (WWF) became involved. They began to study and document the loss of forestland, species, and indigenous cultures. Brazil and other Amazon countries began to respond to all the attention by creating protected areas and environmental laws.

Scientists became the new explorers of the Amazon rain forest. Some searched for new plant and animal species. Some studied rain forest plants in the hope of discovering new medicines. Others studied animal populations and how they worked together. Like the explorer-scientists of centuries past, they faced risks and challenges with creativity.

The high canopy had always been a mystery because it was so hard to reach. Gradually, researchers figured out ways to reach the treetops. Some use a bow and arrow to shoot a rope over a branch and then climb up the rope. Others build ladders or spiral stairways around a tree trunk. Some float over the canopy in hot-air balloons or lightweight airplanes. They also use ski-lift machinery, mountain-climbing equipment, and construction-type cranes.

Respect for the rain forest brought about a new kind of tourism called ecotourism. It gives visitors a way to explore the forest and its people without disrupting them. It also provides employment for local people without extracting their natural resources. Modern-day explorers are still making expeditions of discovery into the forest. They track the routes of early explorers, search for sources of rivers, and seek out undiscovered peoples. Even today, much of the Amazon rain forest remains unexplored. Although more mysteries of the forest are revealed every year, the Amazon may hold some of its secrets forever.

Ecotourists explore the Amazon rain forest without disrupting or harming its natural resources.

FIVE

People of the Forest

The first people in the Amazon region were hunters and gatherers. They came from Siberia, in eastern Asia, but when they arrived is a matter of debate. They may have crossed the Bering Land Bridge that once connected Asia and North America and arrived perhaps 10,000 to 13,000 years ago. Or they may have come by boat as early as 20,000 years ago. Even then, much of the area was tropical rain forest. These people developed diverse ways of life based on hunting, fishing, and gathering plants. They understood how to use and manage forest resources. Over time, they became organized into tribal groups according to language and territory.

Before Europeans arrived, the Amazon region was home to a huge population of indigenous people. Estimates range from 1 million to 10 million people. Gradually, the newcomers decimated the native population. Many Indians were forced into slave labor. Untold thousands died of Europeans' diseases such as measles, smallpox, tuberculosis, and influenza. Others died of overwork, starvation, warfare, and outright murder.

◀ *At one time, there may have been as many as 10 million indigenous people living in the Amazon. Today, that number is closer to 500,000.*

Since the 1960s, roads have crisscrossed native lands and opened the way for miners, ranchers, loggers, and hunters. Fundação Nacional do Índio (FUNAI), Brazil's government agency in charge of Indian affairs, tries to protect the Indians; nevertheless, the deaths have continued. Some Indians even commit suicide when they find their situation hopeless and their way of life lost.

During the 1900s more than ninety tribes disappeared completely. It is difficult to say how many indigenous people live in the Amazon rain forest today. Amazonian countries do not count their indigenous populations. They only make estimates, and they do not separate out native people who live in the Amazon region. Brazil's 2000 census numbered its purely indigenous population at 519,000 people, most of whom lived in the Amazon indigenous reserves. When surveyed, however, more than 734,000 Brazilians identified themselves as indigenous. Other Amazonian countries have smaller indigenous populations, but comparable figures are not available for those countries.

TRADITIONAL WAYS OF LIFE

Indians of the Amazon rain forest have a complex culture. Living in harmony with their environment, they use survival skills that their ancestors developed over thousands of years. Different tribes have different customs, but some traits are common among many groups. To build their huts, they lash saplings together with vines and use palm branches for roofs. They weave baskets and hammocks with sturdy plant fibers.

A typical Indian settlement consists of several families with huts surrounding a central courtyard. Some tribes have chiefs, but most are self-governing. As a group, they make community decisions such as where to hunt and when to move. The shaman is the healer and spiritual leader. He conducts rituals and ceremonial dances and knows the healing powers of various plants. Traditional religious beliefs center on spirits of the forest, earth and sky, animals, and other natural phenomena.

Many tribes paint their bodies, wear tattoos, or use body piercings in the ears, nose, or lower lip. Some groups, although they wear little

Indians from several tribes dance during the Quarup festival to honor their dead.

clothing, adorn themselves with feathers, foliage, and beads. These customs are tied to their spiritual beliefs and their identity as a people.

Men and boys are the hunters, tracking animals by their calls or their footprints. Expert marksmen, they hunt with bows and arrows or blowgun darts. Manioc, or cassava, is a staple food. People gather this starchy root in the forest, grind it, and boil it into a paste. The fruit of the açaí palm, plantains (a type of banana), and other fruit are major sources of food, too. Even children can scramble up tall fruit trees by lashing their ankles together with vines.

Some Indians carry on small-scale farming. Like their ancestors, they understand how the forest works. They cut only enough trees to let sunlight reach the ground. Then they set small fires and scatter the charcoal and ashes around as fertilizer. After farming in one area for a few years, they move on to another spot. They know they must give the soil time to regain its fertility.

In keeping with tradition, men hunt for food for their families using bows and arrows.

More than 230 tribal groups remain in the Amazon rain forest today. Only a few of these tribes live completely traditional lives. The largest groups are the Yanomami on the Brazil–Venezuela border and the Guaraní in southern Mato Grosso state. Other large tribes include the Macuxi of northern Brazil's Roraima state and the Kayapó of Pará and Mato Grosso states. Among the many other indigenous groups are the Kofán and U'wa of Colombia, the Huaorani and Kichwa of Ecuador, the Guaraní and Yuracaré of Bolivia, and the Achuar and Nahua of Peru.

Black Earth

For thousands of years, the Amazon peoples used a form of agriculture called slash-and-char. Using low-intensity, smoldering fires, they burned an area to clear it. Along with the trees and brush, they burned animal and plant wastes and bones. Then they scattered the charcoal from the partially burned trees across the ground. This produced amazingly fertile soil in spots across the forest. Scientists today are studying this soil, called *terra preta*, or "black earth." They believe the forest could become much more fertile if farmers followed the ancient slash-and-char practices.

MAKING CONTACT, DESTROYING LIVES

Loggers are often the first outsiders to make contact with an indigenous group. A typical contact goes the way it did with the Kayapó in the 1980s. Men arrived in pickup trucks full of T-shirts, flashlights, radios, and plastic toys. They gave out the gifts and left. Later they returned, saying the gifts were sold on credit, and it was time to collect on the debt. The Kayapó now owed them the timber that grew on their land. Village leaders were bribed with even larger gifts, such as trucks and stereos. Some leaders made illegal contracts with the loggers and earned handsome profits for themselves. Between 1989 and 1991, the Kayapó had sold $4.3 million worth of timber to logging companies.

The most desirable trees—mahogany—are spaced far apart. Loggers wreck the forest to get to the trees they want. Then farmers or ranchers follow the loggers and burn the trees that are left. For the indigenous people, life in the forest is no longer possible. They are reduced to buying meager food supplies with the little money they receive from the loggers. Logging companies are powerful, and they can easily bribe or threaten judges and other government officials.

Other groups have suffered similar fates. In the 1980s, illegal gold miners entered Yanomami territory near the Venezuelan border. They, too, came bearing gifts. As more miners poured in, they saw the Indians as a nuisance. Violence broke out in the Yanomami Massacre of 1993, which left at least sixteen Indians dead. In 1999 miners discovered diamonds on land reserved for the Cinta Larga tribe. This, too, led to conflicts and bloodshed.

The Uncontacted Tribes

In the vast, unexplored reaches of the forest are Indians who have never had contact with outsiders. The only signs of their existence are footprints and abandoned huts. Some Indians have seen outsiders but avoid all contact with them. They go deeper into the forest, where they can maintain their identity and the life they have led for thousands of years. These mysterious people are known as the uncontacted tribes. In 2007 FUNAI reported the presence of sixty-seven uncontacted tribes in Brazil. They live much as the Indians did when the first European explorers arrived.

FIGHTING BACK

What are the Indians' choices? Some have no choice but to give up. They leave their homes and join white society by getting jobs in the cities and towns. Others live in two worlds. They hold on to some of their traditional ways while maintaining contact with outsiders. They may act as forest guides for tourists and scientists, sell forest products to buy needed goods, or work in health care. Others try to have as little contact with outsiders as possible.

Government measures provide some protections for indigenous people. In 1967 Brazil established FUNAI. Its job is to oversee Indians and to protect their rights and their lands. The new Brazilian constitution of 1988 guaranteed the rights of indigenous peoples to their traditional territories. It called for Indian groups to be identified and their lands to be marked off for their exclusive use.

Today, Brazil has close to six hundred indigenous reserves, covering about one-fifth of the country. Peru, Ecuador, Bolivia, Colombia, and Venezuela have indigenous reserves as well. Still, laws are hard to enforce, and the forest is simply too large to patrol. Illegal activities are widespread, and local officials can be bribed. Some politicians bend the laws in exchange for political favors, while others choose economic development over indigenous rights.

Indigenous people gradually realized they had to fight their own battles. They began forming local associations and political organizations. In Ecuador, Huaorani leader Moi Enomenga organized a political movement in 1990 to resist oil and logging companies. The Confederation of Indigenous Nationalities of Ecuador (CONAIE) is now a strong political force in the country. In Peru, an indigenous organization called Interethnic Association for the Development of the Peruvian Amazon (AIDESEP) is fighting to keep oil companies out of Indian lands.

Some Indians are using computer and satellite technology to protect their lands. The U.S. Agency for International Development (USAID) is training Ecuador's Huaorani people to use global

Oil-drilling operations in the Ecuadorian Amazon severely polluted the region. Indian elders demonstrate for the cleanup of these areas.

positioning system (GPS) devices and digital mapping techniques. With these tools, the people can identify their territory and control intruders. If they discover illegal mining, logging, and farming operations, they can record the exact locations and report them.

The Amazon Conservation Team (ACT) is doing similar work in Suriname, Colombia, and Brazil. It has helped more than a dozen tribes to map their territories. It also trains indigenous people to use Google Earth to view satellite images of their land. Then they can spot illegal airstrips and mines.

CABOCLOS

Caboclos are people of mixed Indian and Portuguese ancestry. Most are descendants of intermarriages during the rubber boom of the late 1800s. They live in scattered settlements along the rivers, far from urban centers, and have little contact with the outside world.

Typically, caboclos carry on small-scale farming. They raise manioc, corn, rice, beans, and watermelons. They collect fruits from a variety of trees—especially the açaí palm—and fish in the rivers and

A caboclo mother and her children canoe on the Amazon.

streams. To protect their activities, caboclos organized associations and began to take part in local environmental politics.

Some caboclos are *seringueiros*, or rubber tappers. In the 1980s Chico Mendes led the seringueiros of Acre state in forming a union. They wanted to protect their rights from land-grabbing cattle ranchers. Mendes was shot and killed by two ranchers in 1988. This brought the rubber tappers to international attention and led to the creation of extractive reserves. These are areas where residents can use and manage forest resources, but they cannot sell any part of the forest.

LANDLESS PEASANTS

Land ownership laws in Brazil give massive tracts of land to wealthy landowners. Many landowners do not farm their land. They just clear it in order to receive funds from the government. Meanwhile, hundreds of thousands of poor people, called landless peasants, have nowhere to farm. Many have settled on landowners' unused farms and ranches. They are called *posseiros*—illegal homesteaders, or settlers with no legal right to the land.

In the 1970s Brazil built the Trans-Amazonian Highway through the heart of the rain forest in Pará and Amazonas states. Landless peasants were encouraged to take the highway into the forest and settle there. In the mad dash for land, tens of thousands of families went there and began farming.

Typically, they used the **slash-and-burn** method of clearing land.

Because the rain forest soil is thin and not very fertile, the settlers grew crops for a short time until the soil was worn out. Then they moved on, often clearing Indians' land.

In Pará state, landless peasants found help from Sister Dorothy Stang, a Roman Catholic nun from Ohio. For more than twenty years, she helped organize landless peasants on the fringe of the rain forest. She worked with them to develop small-scale, **sustainable** farming methods that would not harm the forest.

Stang was a fierce rain forest activist, fighting companies that carried on large-scale deforestation. In the process, she made enemies among ranchers and loggers. In 2005 she was gunned down on the way to a peasants' meeting in a remote forest camp. A wealthy landowner had ordered the execution. Since then, other peasant advocates have been targeted for removal.

Today, landless peasants speak out through Brazil's Landless Workers Movement (*Movimento dos Trabalhadores Rurais Sem Terra*, or MST). This powerful group, which has about 1.5 million members, is fighting for land reforms that would allow them to farm unused land. It also fights abuses by large agricultural firms and conducts educational programs on sustainable farming. Like all people of the forest, these workers can feel powerless in the face of weak laws and big businesses hungry for economic gain. The only way to protect their rights is to fight in ever more sophisticated ways.

SIX

A Forest in Peril

Over the years, about one-fifth of the entire Amazon rain forest has been destroyed. Uncontrolled fires rage through the forest as people clear land for farms and ranches. Bulldozers tear through the wilderness to make roads and to reach valuable trees. Other industrial operations cause flooding or dump chemical wastes into the forest's waterways.

These activities have drastic effects on the rain forest ecosystems. As the natural habitats of animals and plants are demolished, hundreds of species disappear forever. A related problem is the so-called edge effect. Deforestation creates an edge to the forest that exposes it to high winds, brighter light, and dryer conditions. Stand at the edge, and you are struck by the silence. This is because birds, monkeys, and even insects have retreated deeper into the forest. Even in protected areas, their habitat is much smaller than it appears. This edge effect can extend 1,000 feet (300 m) or more into a forest area.

Deforestation also affects the climate, as fires and decaying trees release tons of carbon dioxide into the air. Rainfall decreases, too.

◀ *Fires destroy countless acres of the Amazon rain forest every year.*

Fields and pastures give off less water vapor than forest trees, so much less rain is generated. Scientists fear that more than half the Amazon rain forest may be damaged or reduced to dry grassland by the year 2030.

MAJOR CAUSES OF DEFORESTATION

Cattle ranching is the biggest cause of deforestation in the Amazon region. Unfortunately for the rain forest, ranchers use the slash-and-burn method to clear forestland for cattle pastures. The economic benefits of ranching offer a strong motivation. Brazil is the world's largest exporter of beef. Brazilian beef ends up in supermarkets and fast-food restaurants in the United States, Europe, and elsewhere around the world.

This former rain forest land was cleared to accommodate a cattle ranch in Brazil.

Soybean farming is another threat to the Amazon. Only the United States exports more soybeans than Brazil. U.S. farming has also affected Brazil's soy production. The United States is looking to ethanol as an alternative fuel to petroleum. Since ethanol can be made from corn, more U.S. farmers are switching from soybeans to corn. This creates even more demand for Brazilian soybeans.

Slicing through the Forest

The need to transport products such as soybeans leads to more road construction—and deforestation—in the Amazon. The BR-174 highway cuts through the forest from Manaus, Brazil to Caracas, Venezuela. The partly paved BR-163 is called the soy highway. It slices right through the heart of the rain forest, from Cuiabá near the Bolivian border to Santarém on the banks of the Amazon. Its main purpose is to transport soybeans to Santarém's deep-water port. Another controversial highway is the proposed Trans-Oceanic Highway. It would link Brazilian roads with a highway running over the Andes Mountains to Peruvian ports on the Pacific Ocean. From there, Brazilian soy and other products could reach the markets of Asia. Very little study has been done on the environmental and social impacts of any of these projects.

As pastureland wears out, ranchers move deeper into the forest. Soybean farmers then take over the old pastures. Large, powerful companies control these movements. The major soy companies in the Amazon region are giant, multinational corporations such as Archer Daniels Midland (ADM) and Cargill. Brazil's JBS company is the largest beef producer in the world.

Deforestation Rates

The worst year for deforestation in the Amazon rain forest was August 1994 through August 1995. In that year alone, roughly 11,200 square miles (29,000 square km) of rain forest were cut down. That is an area larger than the state of Massachusetts. The clearing amounted to almost 14 acres (5.7 ha) per minute, around the clock, for a year. The second-worst year was 2003 to 2004, when about 10,000 square miles (25,900 sq km) of forest were cut. Thanks to conservation programs, deforestation reached a low in 2006. However, forest loss shot up again in 2007. Experts say this is due to rising prices for soybeans and beef. With the lure of greater profits, farmers and ranchers are driven to clear more land.

Logging takes its toll on the forest, too. Dozens of Amazon tree species are cut to be sold commercially. The most valuable trees are mahogany, which are made into expensive furniture, wall paneling, boats, and musical instruments. Brazil banned the export of Amazon mahogany in 2001 after finding out that most of the trees were cut illegally from Indian lands. Still, illegal logging continues. Pará state is the main source of mahogany trees and a hotbed of other illegal logging operations.

THE LURE OF GOLD AND OIL

Mining causes a wide range of damages. The gold rush to the Brazil–Venezuela border region began in the late 1970s.

The scope and size of Carajás, the largest iron mine in the Amazon rain forest, can be seen in this aerial view.

Garimpeiros, or illegal gold miners, have wreaked disaster on the region. One source of damage is water pollution. Among Brazil's Yanomami people, mercury used in the gold-mining process poisoned the rivers, endangering both fish and people.

The garimpeiros moved from Brazil to Venezuela where they removed vast amounts of soil and vegetation from the rain forest. This caused soil erosion, clouding the rivers and clogging the country's major hydroelectric dam. Here, too, mercury contaminated the fish and drinking water.

Extracting oil and gas has devastating effects, too. From 1967 through 1992 the Texaco oil company drilled for oil in Ecuador's Amazon rain forest. In the process, it dumped billions of gallons of toxic chemicals into waste pits. The chemicals seeped into rivers and streams and poisoned people's drinking, fishing, and bathing water. Local Indians and peasants began to suffer severe health problems such as cancer and birth defects. They filed a lawsuit against Texaco in 1993. As of 2008, the matter was still not resolved.

In the Peruvian Amazon, the Camisea gas project began in the 1980s. It involved building a natural-gas pipeline. Almost half of the area's Nahua people died of diseases brought by workers. Pollution and soil erosion reduced the rivers' fish supply, which caused malnutrition among the children.

Many other minerals are mined in the rain forest. They include copper, tin, iron ore, manganese, bauxite, lead, and nickel. Mining has a wide range of effects. Wood is cut for charcoal to fuel the mineral-processing ovens. Miners pollute the rivers with litter and human wastes. All around the mining sites, plants and animals are destroyed and human settlements are disrupted.

SPECIES LOSS: A BIODIVERSITY CRISIS

How quickly are species disappearing from the Amazon rain forest? It's hard to say. Many become extinct before they have even been discovered. Some scientists estimate that as many as 50,000 species in the world's rain forests become extinct every year. That amounts to 137 species a day!

Some Amazon species are found nowhere else in the world. Other species have a very small range. They may spend their lives within only a few acres. Once that area is deforested, the species goes, too. Rain forest creatures are especially vulnerable because of their complex interrelationships. One animal species may feed on just one plant. One insect species may live in just one animal's fur. One plant species may be pollinated by just one species of bee. As one species dies out, others disappear, too. Little by little, the ecosystem breaks down.

Larger, more visible creatures are easier to observe, so their populations are easier to track. In the early twenty-first century, more than two hundred animal and plant species in the Amazon region were known to be in danger of extinction. Among them are jaguars, several parrot and macaw species, pink dolphins, manatees, giant river otters, and many monkey species, including golden lion tamarins and spider monkeys.

Macaws are a favorite of poachers. Many macaws die during shipment to other countries.

ANIMALS FOR SALE

Poaching, or illegal hunting, is wiping out many Amazon species. Poachers hunt or trap rare animals, dead or alive. The endangered jaguar is prized for its skin. Crocodile, snake, and lizard skins become shoes, purses, and belts. Some collectors want parrots and macaws as pets, while others just want their feathers or their eggs. Many live animals die in their traps or get crushed or suffocated during shipping. It is estimated that only one in ten animals survives the trip. One batch of birds shipped to Illinois arrived with 12,000 dead birds.

Illegal wildlife passes through a network of middlemen. The ringleaders are wildlife **traffickers**, who make huge profits selling to buyers around the world. Some macaws sell for thousands of dollars, but the original poacher might get a few dollars at best. Wildlife trafficking has connections with the drug trade, too. Some traffickers stuff animals, both dead and alive, with illegal drugs or precious gems.

Brazilian scientists estimate that hunters in the Amazon trap or kill more than 20 million animals a year. Brazil's environmental police—IBAMA (Brazilian Institute of Environment and Renewable Natural Resources)—regularly cracks down on poachers. Still, the practice is so widespread that it's hard to stop.

CONSERVATION EFFORTS

Brazil has found that indigenous reserves are among the best ways to preserve the forest and its biodiversity. When people can manage their own forest resources, they do. The country also has hundreds of other protected areas belonging to national, state, and private owners. Satellite images show that deforestation and forest fires are drastically lower within these areas and the indigenous reserves.

In 2002 Brazil joined with the World Wildlife Fund (WWF) and other organizations to create the Amazon Region Protected Area (ARPA) program. Its goal is to set up eighty reserves and parks, covering a total area the size of California. As part of this program, Brazil established Tumucumaque National Park, the largest tropical forest park in the world.

Rising rates of deforestation in 2007 alarmed the Brazilian government. In 2008 it launched an operation called Arc of Fire. In this

Tumucumaque National Park

In 2002 Brazil established Tumucumaque National Park in the northern state of Amapá. At 15,000 square miles (39,000 sq km), it is larger than the entire country of Belgium. Jaguars, monkeys, and thousands of other species make their homes there. Many of the park's animal species live nowhere else in the world. Scientists are just beginning to study the diverse wildlife there.

massive crackdown on illegal logging, hundreds of armed troops shut down logging sites. In its first three months alone, the operation seized enough illegally logged wood to fill 1,500 trucks.

Other countries are protecting their rain forest areas, too. For example, Peru maintains the Manú Biosphere Reserve. It stretches across 7,000 square miles (18,130 sq km) of southeastern Peru. Scientists consider it the most biologically diverse ecosystem on Earth. The United Nations Educational, Scientific, and Cultural Organization (UNESCO) has named the reserve a World Heritage Site. That means it is of great value to the entire global community.

Dozens of international conservation groups are also working to save the forest and its wildlife. Just one example is the Primate

Rehabilitation Center near Manaus. It houses monkeys confiscated from wildlife traffickers. The center cares for the monkeys, makes sure they are healthy, and returns them to the rain forest.

The Future: Having It Both Ways?

The countries of the Amazon region are poor, their populations are growing fast, and the need for economic development is strong. As one local official said, "Why are people cutting down forest? Because they like to? No. Brazil is a poor country. We have to develop."

Ideally, development and conservation can work out ways to coexist. According to Dr. Betty Meggers, an archaeologist who studies early Amazonian cultures, "The choice need not lie between irreversible devastation and no exploitation at all." She points out that early peoples both utilized and preserved the forest for thousands of years. If we learn from their methods, we can sustain the forest environment for years to come.

◄ *The Amazon rain forest is one of the most diverse natural wonder of the world. Worldwide conservation efforts aim to provide sustainability for the region, for all that live there, and for future generations.*

Glossary

biodiversity   the number and types of organisms within a region

continental   relating to or occurring on a continent, one of the seven large land masses on Earth

deforestation   the removal of trees to convert forestland to a nonforest use

ecosystem   an environment in which living things function together as a unit

evaporation   the process of changing from a liquid to a gas

floodplain   an area that is regularly flooded by a rise in river or lake levels

habitat   the natural environment in which a species lives

indigenous   original; living in an area before recorded history

silt   particles of soil carried by a river

slash-and-burn   a method of clearing land by cutting and burning trees and other vegetation

sustainable   describing a way of using resources without harming them for future use

symbiotic   describing a close relationship between two organisms that benefits both

toxic   poisonous

traffickers   smugglers; dealers who buy, sell, or transport goods illegally

transpiration   the release of moisture from leaves in the form of water vapor

tributaries   small rivers that empty into a larger river

vapor   the gaseous state of a solid or liquid

Fast Facts

Name: Amazon rain forest

Other names: Amazonia, Amazon Basin

First European contact: 1500, Vicente Yáñez Pinzón (Spanish)

Countries: Brazil (60%), Peru (16%), Bolivia (12%), Colombia, Ecuador (2%), Venezuela, French Guiana, Suriname, Guyana

Major cities: Manaus, Belém (Brazil); Iquitos, Pucallpa (Peru); Tena (Ecuador)

Languages spoken: Indigenous languages, Portuguese (in Brazil), Spanish (in other countries)

Borders: Andes Mountains on the west, Atlantic Ocean on the east, Guiana Highlands on the north, Brazilian Highlands on the south

Area of river basin: About 2.5 million square miles (6.5 million sq km)

Dimensions, north to south: About 1,550 miles (2,500 km)

Dimensions, east to west: About 2,240 miles (3,600 km)

Major rivers: Amazon, Solimões, Rio Negro, Madeira, Purus, Japurá

Highest point: Pico da Neblina (9,822 feet/2,994 m), near the Brazil–Venezuela border

Average elevation: Less than 330 feet (100 m) above sea level

Average temperature: 79 °F (26 °C)

Average precipitation: About 90 inches (230 cm) a year; regional variations, about 60 to 120 inches (150 to 300 cm) a year

Population: Indigenous people, 519,000 (2000 est., Brazil); other residents, 21 million (2004 est., Brazil); other countries, (NA)

Ethnic groups: More than 230 indigenous groups, including Guaraní, Yanomami, Macuxi, Kayapó, Huaorani, U'wa, Achuar, and Nahua; *caboclos* (mixed Indian and Portuguese ancestry); other mixed-ancestry peoples

Major animals:

Mammals: jaguars, tapirs, sloths, bats, dolphins, manatees, river otters; many monkey species, including howler monkeys, capuchin monkeys, spider monkeys, tamarins, and marmosets

Birds: parrots, macaws, toucans

Reptiles: anacondas, emerald tree boas, lizards, caimans

Amphibians: frogs, toads, turtles

Fish: piranhas, pirarucus, catfish

Insects: many species, including bees, butterflies, moths, beetles, termites, and ants

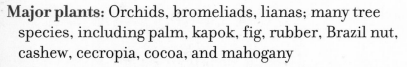

Tamarin

Major plants: Orchids, bromeliads, lianas; many tree species, including palm, kapok, fig, rubber, Brazil nut, cashew, cecropia, cocoa, and mahogany

Protected areas: Indigenous reserves, extractive reserves, nature parks

Major nature parks: Jaú National Park, Tumucumaque National Park (Brazil); Manú National Park, Tambopata National Park (Peru); Cuyabeno Wildlife Reserve, Yasuni National Park (Ecuador); Madidi National Park (Bolivia)

Economic resources: Pastureland, cropland, timber, latex, fruits, nuts, medicinal plants, fish, gold, petroleum, natural gas, other minerals, water for hydroelectric power

Bromeliad

Greatest threats: Ranching, farming, mining, logging, hunting, road construction, forest fires, oversettlement, economic development

Environmental issues: Deforestation, soil erosion, water pollution, disruption of carbon–oxygen exchange, habitat loss, species loss

Cultural issues: Loss of indigenous lands, decline in indigenous population and culture, loss of other subsistence cultures

Find Out More

BOOKS

Aloian, Molly, and Bobbie Kalman. *Rainforest Food Chains*. New York: Crabtree, 2007.

Ganeri, Anita. *Living in the Amazon Rain Forest*. Chicago: Raintree, 2008.

Honovich, Nancy. *The Field Guide to Rain Forest Animals: Explore the Amazon Jungle*. Berkeley, CA: Silver Dolphin Books, 2008.

Johnson, Jinny, and Nalini Nadkarni. *Rain Forest*. Boston: Kingfisher, 2006.

Platt, Richard, and Rupert van Wyk (illustrator). *The Vanishing Rainforest*. London: Frances Lincoln, 2007.

Reynolds, Jan. *Amazon Basin* (Vanishing Cultures). New York: Lee & Low Books, 2007.

Sen, Benita. *Rainforest Creatures*. New York: PowerKids Press, 2008.

WEBSITES

The Amazon Rainforest
www.rainforests.mongabay.com/amazon/
An extensive survey of the Amazon rain forest—its wildlife, ecosystems, forest layers, people, and environmental issues.

Indigenous Peoples in Brazil
www.socioambiental.org/pib/english/whwhhow/index.shtm
To learn about Brazil's indigenous peoples, their territories, and their ways of life.

Save the Amazon Rainforest
www.amazon-rainforest.org/
To find out about the Amazon rain forest's importance, products, history, wildlife, nature preserves, and destructive activities.

Index

Page numbers in **boldface** are illustrations and charts.

ABOUT THE AUTHOR

Ann Heinrichs is the author of more than two hundred books for children and young adults. They cover a range of subjects, from U.S. and world history, geography, and cultures to biography and grammar. She has written Nature's Wonders, *The Nile*, *The Sahara*, and *Mount Everest* for Marshall Cavendish. An avid traveler, Heinrichs has made her way through most of the United States, as well as Europe, the Middle East, Africa, and East Asia. Her travels have also taken her to the temperate rain forests of the Pacific Northwest and the tropical jungles of Mexico.